Thank you for a book to read

Patricia & Victor Smeltzer

A LION BOOK

Sarah went to the bookshop
to choose a book to read.

"Thank you, **bookseller,**
for this book to read,"
said Sarah.

"Don't thank me,"
said the bookseller.
"I only sold you the book.
You must thank the one
who wrote it."

So Sarah went to say
"Thank you" to ...

... the **author.**

"Thank you, **author,**
for my book,"
said Sarah.

"Don't thank me,"
said the author.
"I wrote the story
but someone else
had to make the book.
You must thank the one
who made it."

So Sarah went to say
"Thank you" to ...

... the **publisher.**

"Thank you, **publisher,**
for my book,"
said Sarah.

"Don't thank me,"
said the publisher.
"I only planned
the making of the book.
You must thank the one
who printed it."

So Sarah went to say
"Thank you" to ...

... the **printer.**

"Thank you, **printer,**
for my book,"
said Sarah.

"Don't thank me,"
said the printer.
"I needed paper
on which to print the book.
You must thank the ones
who brought me the paper."

So Sarah went to say
"Thank you" to ...

... the **carriers.**

"Thank you, **carriers,**
for my book,"
said Sarah.

"Don't thank us,"
said the carriers.
"We only brought the rolls
of paper to the printer.
You must thank the ones
who gave us the paper."

So Sarah went to say
"Thank you" to ...

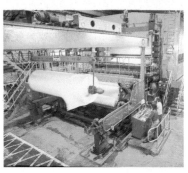
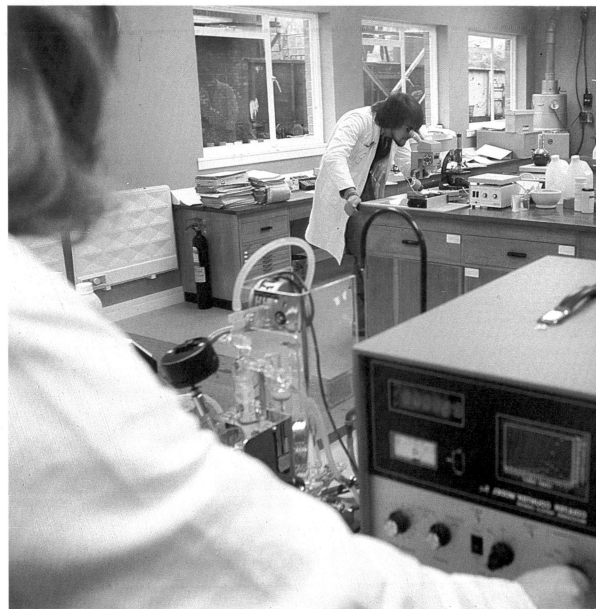

"Thank you,
paper mill workers,
for my book," said Sarah.

"Don't thank us,"
said the workers.
"We only made the paper
from wood pulp.
You must thank the ones
who gave us the wood
to crush into pulp."

So Sarah went to say
"Thank you" to ...

... the **logs.**

"Thank you, **logs,**
   for my book," said Sarah.

"Don't thank us," said the logs.
"We only floated down the river
   to the paper mill. We were
   once part of other things.
   You must thank them."

So Sarah went to say
"Thank you" to ...

... the **trees** in the forest.

"Thank you, **trees,**
   for my book,"
   said Sarah.

"Don't thank us,"
   said the trees.
"We needed other things
   to make us grow.
   You must thank them."

So Sarah went to say
"Thank you" to ...

... the **soil, rain** and **sun.**

"Thank you, **soil, rain** and **sun,**
for my book," said Sarah.

"Don't thank us," they all said.
"You must thank the one
who made us."

So Sarah said "Thank you" to ...

... **God.**

Sarah said this prayer:

"Thank you, **God,**
for making
the **soil, rain** and **sun,**

and for the **trees** and **logs;**

Thank you, **God,**
for the **paper mill workers,**

and the **carriers,**

and the **printer;**

Thank you, **God,**
for the **publisher,**

and the **author,**

and for the **bookseller;**

Thank you, **God,**
for a book to read,

and thank you for helping me
to learn to read.

Amen."